The Greatest Gardening ·TIPS· in the World®

by

Steve Brookes

Illustrated by Graham Robson

Public Eye Publications

A Public Eye Publications Book

www.thegreatestintheworld.com

Illustrations:
Graham Robson, 'Drawing the Line'
info@dtline.co.uk

Cover design:
pentacorbig:
book & information graphic design
www.pentacorbig.co.uk

Layout design:
Bloomfield Ltd.

Copy editor:
Bronwyn Robertson
www.theartsva.com

Series creator / editor:
Steve Brookes

First published in 2004 by
Public Eye Publications, PO Box 3182
Stratford-upon-Avon, Warwickshire CV37 7XW

This edition published in 2005 by
Public Eye Publications, PO Box 3182
Stratford-upon-Avon, Warwickshire CV37 7XW

A CIP catalogue record for this book is available from the British Library
ISBN 1-905151-06-3

Printed and bound by Biddles Ltd., Kings Lynn, Norfolk, PE30 4LS

To
Anne, Mum & Joy for their love and support.

To
Joe, Laura & Amy for putting up with
a workaholic dad!

To
My Dad, who would have been so proud and
would have shown it to everyone!

Contents

A few words from Steve . . .

I began writing this book over 30 years ago at the very frost tender age of . . . well let's just say I was in short trousers with a great love of plants and nature! I began collecting gardening tips then and writing them down in old school exercise books, intending, one day, to publish them as a great horticultural work. Some tips were imparted to me by my grandfather and other wise old sages of the gardening world (no pun intended!) whose paths crossed mine on my green and pleasant journey through adolescence.

The dramatic streak within me resulted in the offer of a trial with the prestigious Royal Shakespeare Company when I was 15, but I was undeterred and resolved to pursue a career in horticulture. My enthusiasm for gardening was fuelled in my late teens by a wonderful TV gardener with a soft Yorkshire accent and a passion for plants that captivated me - Geoffrey Smith. I knew then that gardening was to be my vocation. As my career grew, so did the number of amazing tips I had collected. Eventually I decided to test the tips to see how many really did work and why.

Those that did (and there were many!) are included, at last, in this book. Some of the tips are common sense, some are amusing, and others seem, well, just so wacky that they couldn't possibly work, but they do. With some, I have tried to explain in more detail exactly how and why they work. If you need further convincing - just try them! I must also point out that it was a twang of nostalgia that led me to stick with the old imperial measurements in the text. There's not a millimetre in sight! Those who remember times when a foot was 12 inches and a meter was something the gasman read will know just where I'm coming from!

I really hope that you find reading and using the tips and advice as interesting and rewarding as it has been for me collecting them! The tips have been shown to work on many occasions but there can be no guarantee that they will work every time as all gardens and conditions can vary. They are, however, fun, rewarding, money saving, and environmentally friendly and are considered by me to be 'The Greatest Gardening Tips in the World'! Writing this book of gardening tips has fuelled my enthusiasm for publishing more fun and useful tips books for other important areas of our lives. By bringing on board home & leisure authors who are each an expert in their field 'The Greatest Tips in the World' series has been born. You can see the other titles on pages 158 and 159.

Have fun and enjoy life.

The Greatest Gardening Tips in the World

Half a dried cowpat gives a blooming good hanging basket!

Some gardening tips may seem a little odd and raise an eyebrow of suspicion, but can really work well. This is one such beauty and the results are amazing...

To keep the annual flowers in your hanging baskets and containers looking wonderful, crumble up a dried cowpat and mix into the compost before planting. Approximately half a dinner plate sized pat is perfect for a 14" basket or tub. Wear gloves, of course, but amazingly there is no smell!

Drainpipe sections make great plant supports

Certain plants such as runner beans, clematis and sweet peas, benefit from support from the time they are planted. Tying them to canes when they are young can be fiddly and cause damage to the thin stems. A really good alternative is to use a section of plastic drainpipe cut to a length about 2" higher than the plant. Slide the pipe gently over the plant and push about 2" into the soil. Not only will this provide support but will also prevent wind damage to the tender plant AND will deter those pesky slugs and snails. Good eh?

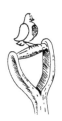

Save your strawberries with the help of a friendly toad

Slugs and snails can decimate a strawberry patch of fruit overnight. A good natural solution is to use one of nature's most voracious nocturnal hunters – the toad! Securely net off your strawberry bed and introduce a toad into the netted area. By ensuring that he cannot escape and that there is always a bowl of fresh water available, your warty friend will happily remain there all summer, making short work of the slugs and snails. Thankfully, toads are carnivores so he will leave the juicy strawberries alone!

Wash day blues for slugs and snails

A short-lived but very effective deterrent for slugs and snails is washing powder. Keep a box of the cheap, own brand sort for those emergencies when you have none of the more permanent items from other tips in this book. A handful of washing powder around a plant will stop the little devils by clogging up their slime glands. They are literally stopped in their tracks! Unfortunately, after the first shower of rain the effect is gone, so treat it as a temporary measure.

Couch grass cleared by territorial tomatoes!

Another one of those tips that no one really knows why it works. If your garden has a patch of couch grass that is proving difficult to get rid of, then sow some tomato seeds in the middle of it in early spring. The tomato seedlings will grow and the couch grass will have disappeared! It seems the two can't compete and the tomato plants win every time. Some scientists think that a chemical produced by the tomato plant roots kills the couch grass. Who cares – as long as it works?!

Protect those old garden tools

I think you will agree that old gardening tools, passed down from generation to generation, give lovely nostalgic connotations of bygone gardening days. Sadly they can become rusted if not cleaned thoroughly after each use. The solution, according to TV gardener Geoffrey Smith, is to make up a 'pontica' bucket – a bucket filled with sharp sand soaked with old engine oil. After use, the trusty old spade, fork or trowel is plunged vigorously up and down into the sand. Any remains of soil are removed by the sand and the tool is left with a thin coating of rust preventing oil. Magic!

Pot protection from slugs and snails

Even plants in containers are not safe from the nocturnal nibbling of hungry slugs and snails. Preventing them from actually reaching the object of their desire – your prize plants – is easier than you think. A 2" wide barrier around the pot is usually enough. To make this barrier use either Vaseline, WD-40 (the water repellent spray), or double-sided sticky tape. If using the spray, ensure that you protect the plants with newspaper. The slugs and snails don't like the stickiness of the Vaseline or tape and they seem to hate the WD-40.

Steve's favourite 20 'winter-wonder' flowering trees and shrubs . . .

Chaenomeles speciosa (Ornamental Quince)

Chimonanthus praecox (Wintersweet)

Cornus mas (Cornelian Cherry)

Corylopsis (Fragrant Winterhazel)

Corylus avellana 'Contorta' (Corkscrew Hazel)

Daphnae bholua 'Jaqueline Postill'

Erica carnea 'Pink Spangles' (Winter Flowering Heather)

Garrya elliptica (Silk Tassel Bush)

Hamamelis x intermedia 'Jelena' (Witch Hazel)

Hamamelis mollis (Chinese Witch Hazel)

Jasminum nudiflorum (Winter Jasmine)

Lonicera fragrantissima (Honeysuckle)

Lonicera purpusii 'Winter Beauty' (Honeysuckle)

Lonicera standishii (Honeysuckle)

Mahonia 'Charity'

Parrotia persica (Persian ironwood)

Prunus x subhirtella 'Autumnalis' (Rosebud cherry)

Rhododendron dauricum 'Midwinter'

Viburnum x bodnantense 'Dawn'

Viburnum farreri

Stinging nettles are not the bad-boy weeds you think they are

Don't be too hasty in ridding your garden of every stinging nettle you see. Many butterflies will only lay their eggs in the protective stinging foliage of a nettle so leave a few around to increase the numbers of these valuable pollinating insects. Nettles are also packed full of nitrogen so any you do remove will be prime fillet steak to the compost heap, helping to activate the breakdown process and giving you a much better quality compost. In fact, actively look to scrounge nettles from neighbours and friends for this purpose. They may think you are bonkers but you'll have the last laugh!

African violets like it dry and dull

Sometimes plants really amaze you with their requirements for success. African violets hate being wet and don't like sunlight much either! Only water them when the leaves begin to wilt (yes - that dry!) and stand them by the glass on a north-facing windowsill. Given these conditions they will flourish and flower for much longer.

No more wobbly lines of carrots!

A very easy way to make a perfectly straight seed drill in the vegetable patch is to use a 1" diameter broom handle. First, prepare the soil to a level surface, firm with your feet and finish by lightly raking the top 1"of soil to loosen it. Then gently lay the broom handle onto the soil and press to the required depth. When removed, you have the perfect seed drill!

Line your pots and save on watering

Large terracotta pots always look wonderful on the patio but, because of the porous nature of clay, the compost in them tends to dry out quickly. Avoid this problem at planting time, by lining the pots with plastic carrier bags, making sure that they are hidden under the top surface of the compost. Water loss from the pot is considerably reduced.

A green tomato makes hand cleaning easy

Green stains on your hands after removing the side shoots of your tomato plants can be really difficult to remove. Here's the easy way... before washing your stained hands with soap, cut a green tomato in half and rub the cut side vigorously over the stains. The stains are then easily removed with normal washing. The same plant that caused the problem has helped you solve it!

An organic solution to rose mildew

Mildew on roses is often a difficult disease to control unless you want to resort to frequent chemical sprayings. Try this – it's worked on many occasions and is totally organic . . .

Mix 1 tablespoon of baking powder with ¼ pint of milk and add a teaspoon of cooking oil. Stir thoroughly and pour into a hand sprayer. Liberally coat both sides of the leaves of the affected rose. The baking powder and the milk are the effective ingredients and the oil just helps the mixture stick to the leaves.

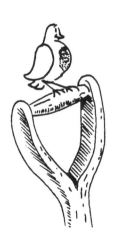

Egg Box – home for overwintering ladybirds

Ladybirds are one of the garden's most useful predatory insects and will happily feed for hours on troublesome greenfly. To ensure that there are ladybirds resident in your garden from early spring you need to provide them with a safe haven in which to overwinter. The best thing is an old egg box, opened out and pushed, upside down, into a hedge, under a shed or somewhere else where it will be relatively dry and undisturbed through the winter months. The ladybirds will find the egg compartments both warm, dry and a safe refuge from predators.

Silicone sealant gives super support

Climbing plants such as clematis, honeysuckle and jasmine can be firmly held to a wall or fence using clear silicone sealant bought from the DIY store. Simply decide where you want the stem of the plant to go and put a 1" diameter blob of sealant at the appropriate place on the wall or fence. Allow about 10 minutes for setting then gently push the stem of the climber right into the middle of the blob of sealant. The climber will be held firmly against the support and the sealant will stretch to cope with the expanding stem. If you ever need to reposition the climber or temporarily remove it for painting or repairs then simply prize off the sealant and carefully cut it off the plant stem. When you are ready just reaffix with more sealant. This natty method of plant support does away with the bother of nails, hooks, wires etc… and is almost invisible.

A two-pronged attack for an ant free existence

Ants are perhaps the most disliked of any garden pest because they have the audacity to come into your house as well! Try as you may with regular ant powders, they never seem to do the whole job. That's because they kill by contact and although the ants on the surface succumb, the real culprit is sitting pretty in her protective subterranean domain – the queen! She is happily churning out new ants to replace those you kill above ground. Killing her is the secret to a respite from annoying ants because if she dies the colony cannot survive. Killing the queen isn't easy. She is fed by the worker ants who will not feed her anything they realise is dangerous.

The trick is to dupe the ants into feeding the queen poison by lacing it with the one thing that disrupts their senses and sends them into ant heaven – sugar. And the one thing that is certain death to an ant is naturally occurring borax, available in crystal form as a laundry cleaning aid. Mix one part sugar with one part borax crystals and sprinkle where you can see the ants appearing. The borax sticks to the sugar and the ants are oblivious to its presence. Ants are not allowed to eat until they have fed the queen so they happily stuff her full of the mixture and she quickly expires. Now the colony is in complete disarray without a queen. The ants soon coming running out of the nest, which is when you knock them off with ant powder, or a friendly anteater if you want to be really environmentally friendly!

For ripe tomatoes – go bananas!

Towards the end of the growing season, tomatoes both inside and out, become very slow to ripen. This is due to a reduction in the intensity of the sunlight, which needs to be high to trigger the production of the gas, ethylene, in the tomato skins to ripen them (all very technical this, isn't it?!). What you need to know is how to ripen the green tomatoes. The answer is simple – a pound of bananas! Hang the bananas individually amongst the tomato plants. The bananas' skins give off loads of ethylene as they quickly ripen and before you know it any reluctant green tomatoes have gone red!

Don't waste those excess drips

Hanging baskets can dry out very quickly due to the effects of the sun and the wind. The rule of thumb is to water a hanging basket until excess water runs out of the bottom. Great advice but what happens to the excess water? It is wasted. A simple tip is to put an empty bucket under the basket before watering to collect the run off and use elsewhere.

Keep cats at bay with tea bags and muscle spray!

Cats! A word that can instil dread into many a gardener. Newly tilled soil is their perfect litter tray and the deposits made are not a welcome find - especially if you don't wear gardening gloves! An easy way to keep cats away from any area of the garden is by drying out used tea bags and spraying them with a muscle rub spray, such as 'Ralgex'. The tea bags can then be buried about $1/2$" deep over the soil area where the cats scratch, or left in those corners of the garden where the cats mark their territory. The cats hate the smell and will keep well away! Being oily, the muscle spray is not easily washed off by the rain and the deterrent will last for a good two weeks, by which time the cat has found another, more convenient, convenience!

Steve's choice of formal and informal hedging plants . . .

Formal:

Buxus sempervirens (Box)
Carpinus betulus (Hornbeam)
Fagus sylvatica (Common Beech)
Ilex aquifolium (Holly)
Prunus laurocerasus (Cherry Laurel)
Prunus lusitanica (Portugal Laurel)
Taxus baccata (Yew)
Thuja plicata (Western Red Cedar

Informal:

Acer campestre (Field Maple)
Berberis darwinii (Barberry)
Berberis stenophylla (Barberry)
Chaenomeles speciosa (Ornamental Quince)
Cotoneaster simonsii
Escallonia rubra var. macrantha
Elaeagnus macrophylla
Euonymus japonicus
Forsythia species
Photinia fraseri 'Red Robin'
Pyracantha species (Firethorn)
Rosa rugosa (Hedgehog Rose)
Rosa 'Felicia'
Spirea billardii 'Triumphans'
Viburnum tinus

Ring the changes in your flower border

If you can find them at boot fairs and junkyards, try to get hold of some of the metal bands from around wooden beer barrels or wine casks. You can often find different sizes and they make attractive circular planting areas for bulbs and sowings of annual flower seeds. Place the rings on the soil surface in your chosen pattern and plant or sow into them as usual. When the bulbs or seedlings start to appear you can remove the metal rings and store for use next year.

Assault those despicable dandelions

If you want to get rid of those odd dandelions in your lawn but don't want to spray weed killer, then a little table salt poured into the centre of the plant will do the trick. This will slowly burn out the heart of the weed.

Suspend your onions in stockings for perfect storage

Storing onions over the winter can be a mouldy experience if they touch each other! A good circulation of air around the bulbs is needed and this can be easily achieved by storing the onions in old tights or stockings. Just drop an onion in and tie the material above it into a knot then put another onion in, tie a knot and so forth. When you need an onion simply cut the lowest one off just below the knot.

Space saving cuttings with a freezer bag and a clothes peg

Here is a great way of taking numerous cuttings without utilising any bench space at all. Take your cuttings in the usual way, cutting at an angle just below a leaf joint, making the piece of stem about 4" to 5" long. Remove any flower buds and, with the exception of pelargoniums and any other very succulent stemmed plants, dip the cut end into a little hormone rooting powder. Now push the cutting into the corner of a clear plastic freezer bag containing about 2" deep of well-moistened good quality multi-purpose compost mixed with a little sharp sand for extra drainage. Loosely gather the bag opening and with a clothes peg, hang to a previously fixed string line across the greenhouse, potting shed, conservatory or anywhere that is brightly lit but can be protected from full sun. Those cuttings that take will produce white roots at the side of the compost in the bag and can then be carefully removed and potted up. Those that do not show signs of rooting can be discarded with nothing lost apart from a bit of compost. Taking cuttings in this way means that you can really experiment and try all sorts of plants. There should be no need to add further water to the bag because what is there will condense back into the compost and, providing you have gathered the neck of the bag loosely, fresh air can still reach the cutting.

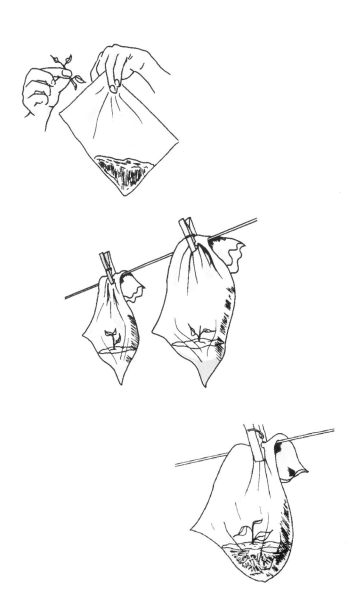

Sort out those loose ends!

An old jam jar with a hole punched through the lid makes a great storage container for those unravelled balls of garden twine or string. Put the ball into the jar and poke the free end of the twine through the hole in the lid. Replace the lid and you have a clever little dispenser.

Impressive autumn masterpiece

Collect nice examples of colourful autumn leaves and press them between some heavy books for a few weeks. Then buy a cheap clip picture frame and arrange the leaves on the backboard. Clip the glass back on and you have an inexpensive and individual wall decoration.

Plants prefer a warm evening bath

Evening is by far the best time for watering plants. Some of them, however, are more sensitive to chills than others and watering with very cold water on a spring or autumn evening can occasionally cause problems. To avoid this, simply fill your watering cans in the morning and put them in the shed, greenhouse or garage. By evening the water will have warmed up and will be at a more acceptable temperature for your plants.

Roll out the red carpet for a good crop of beans!

Avoid the flowers on runner and French beans falling before they have set by ensuring that the plants never run short of water. To keep the soil from drying out a good tip is to lay strips of old carpet around the plants, or even lay the carpet down first and cut holes for planting or sowing. This carpet 'mulch' will also warm the soil for faster germination of seeds and growth of the plants.

Banish those bulb growing blues with a handful of sand

A poor show from your spring flowering bulbs can often be avoided at planting time. Bulbs are just lunch boxes full of food so don't worry about feeding until after they have finished flowering. What is important is drainage and making sure that there are no air gaps beneath the bulb. Both these problems can be sorted out with nothing more than a handful of sharp sand placed in the hole at planting time. Pressed gently into the sand the bulb will be able to cope with a wet winter and any air gaps will be filled to allow the roots to grow without a struggle. A word on planting depths: a good rule of thumb is to make the hole twice the depth of the bulb. Planting too deep can result in a 'blind' plant, which refuses to flower, and too shallow can provide easy pickings for the hungry squirrel!

Garden with soap for that manicured look!

If you are one of those gardeners who prefers not to wear gloves when gardening, then you will relate to this problem: the 'grubby nail' scenario. After a day in the garden you will spend an eternity scrubbing to remove the soil embedded deep under your nails, in preparation for that special night out. Use this tip for crystal clear nails every time. Before you go out into the garden run your nails firmly over the surface of a bar of soap. When you come to wash your hands later the soap from under your nails can be easily removed and not one speck of dirt will remain!

Keep those secateurs within easy reach

Never go into the garden without a pair of secateurs in your hand. Nine times out of ten you will find something that you need to clip, prune or deadhead and you will have to go back and get your secateurs. Keep a spare pair on the kitchen windowsill and get into the habit of always taking them with you.

Recycle those old inner tubes into the best plant ties

Without doubt the best universal plant ties, especially for roses, are thin strips of cycle inner tube. There is nothing better! Apart from being almost impossible to break they give a bit to allow for movement in windy conditions. Local cycle repair shops are throwing out old inner tubes by the dozen and should be more than happy to give you a few. Cut them into various lengths and widths for a multitude of garden uses.

An old pair of tights + a pile of sheep droppings = wonderful liquid plant food!

One of the most rewarding gardening tasks is making your own plant food and saving yourself a fortune at the garden centre. Years ago old gardeners used to stuff pigeon droppings into the foot end of a pair of stockings. These 'smelly feet' were then steeped in the water butt or a bucket of water for a couple of weeks to make a wonderful liquid plant feed for the whole garden. Today pigeons are not kept so much but a similar rich liquid feed can be achieved by using sheep droppings collected on a romantic Sunday stroll in the country! Remember that these 'neat' animal manures are too strong to be used directly on the soil. Keep one water butt as your food factory and use every couple of weeks on your plants.

Steve's basket of 20 beautiful berrying shrubs . . .

Ampelopsis brevipendunculata

Berberis darwinii (Barberry)

Callicarpa bodinieri var. giraldii 'Profusion' (Beauty Berry)

Clerodendrum bungei

Cotoneaster frigidus 'Cornubia'

Crataegus monogyna (Common Hawthorn)

Euonymus europaeus 'Red Cascade' (Spindleberry)

Gaultheria mucronata (Prickly Heath)

Ilex aquifolium (Holly)

Leycesteria formosa (Pheasant Berry)

Mahonia aquifolium (Oregon Grape)

Prunus laurocerastus (Cherry Laurel)

Pyracantha coccinea 'Orange Glow' (Firethorn)

Rosa rugosa (Hedgehog Rose)

Sambucus nigra (Elderberry)

Skimmia fortunei

Symphoricarpos albus (Snowberry)

Vaccinium ovatum (Box Blueberry)

Viburnum davidii

Viburnum opulus (Guelder rose)

Containerised carrots for a year-round harvest

Freshly pulled carrots can be enjoyed throughout the year, even on Christmas Day. Choose a short rooted variety and sow thinly about 1/2" deep in used 4 litre ice cream containers filled with a free draining soil-based compost. Ensure that the container has drainage holes in the bottom and keep in a well-lit, cool, spare room or frost-free greenhouse. OK you won't get a vast quantity of carrots this way but you have the thrill of an out of season crop!

Take a look at the origins of your species!

You don't need a degree in botany to be able to grow a range of plants from around the world – just a good atlas. With detailed knowledge of the countries from which the plants originate you can mimic their natural growing conditions and achieve great success. Lavender and many other herbs, for instance, come from a Mediterranean climate, so full sun and sandy, free draining soil is the order of the day. Not only does this information make your gardening more rewarding and enjoyable but you also discover new plants to grow.

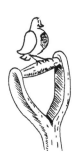

Use sunflowers to invite the hoverflies for a greenfly feast!

Hoverflies are some of the most useful insects in your garden because the adults and the larvae are voracious eaters of greenfly. In fact the hoverfly will actively look for colonies of greenfly in which to lay its eggs. Yellow flowers are a great attraction for this friendly predator, which likes to hover at different levels in the garden looking for nectar on which to feed. The best way to keep hoverflies in your garden is to plant different heights of sunflowers from 'Dwarf Yellow Spray' at 18" right up to the massive 'Russian Giant' at more than 10'. You will benefit from the fabulous flowers, the antics of the birds and squirrels trying to get the seeds in the autumn, but best of all – your built in greenfly control!

45

Turn vacuum cleaner fluff into tip-top tomato food

Tomato plants are hungry little devils and particularly fussy eaters! Apart from the normal plant foods they crave for trace elements and minerals such as iron, manganese, magnesium, calcium, copper, boron and sulphur. These 'extras' give the plants and their fruit added health, quality and taste as well as resistance to disease and deficiency symptoms. Trace element feeds are available but the best source for all of these requirements is hidden under your feet – vacuum cleaner fluff! One handful per week mulched into the soil or compost at the base of the tomato plant gives amazing results – healthier plants as well as better tasting fruit with thinner skins and a resistance to splitting.

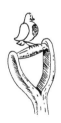

Increase your berry bonanza with a homemade collector

When picking blackberries and the like, having two hands free means more berries picked in the time you have. A large empty plastic milk container, bottom cut off, turned upside down and held round your waist with a belt through the handle makes a brilliant berry collector!

Scary film for the birds

A single old, discarded video cassette can be easily recycled into hundreds of bird scarers to protect newly emerging seedlings. Pull out 2' lengths of the tape and tie to canes. The slightest breeze will blow the tape about and the shiny side will catch the light to further startle the birds.

Fast solution to burying slow-release fertiliser

Don't get your fingernails all messy trying to push those cone-shaped bundles of slow-release fertiliser pellets into hanging baskets and tubs. Instead use an apple corer to make a hole – it is just the right size and you can easily pop the plug of compost back in the hole after dropping in the slow-release pellets.

Steve's 20 favourite trees for the smaller garden . . .

Acer griseum (Paper Bark Maple)

Acer pensylvanicum (Snakeskin Bark Maple)

Aesculus pavia 'Atrosanguinea' (Dark Red Buckeye)

Amelanchier lamarkii or Amelanchier laevis (Snowy Mespilus)

Aralia elata (Japanese Angelica Tree)

Arbutus unedo (Strawberry Tree)

Betula pendula 'Fastigiata' (Silver Birch)

Cornus florida 'Spring Song' (Flowering Dogwood)

Corylus avellana 'Contorta' (Corkscrew Hazel)

Crataegus persimilis 'Prunifolia' (Hawthorn)

Laburnum alpinum (Scots Laburnum)

Malus 'Red Jade' *or Malus* 'John Downie' (Crab Apples)

Malus domestica 'Katja' (Desert Apple)

Prunus 'Kursar' (Ornamental Cherry)

Prunus x subhirtella 'Autumnalis' (Winter Cherry)

Prunus subhirtella 'Pendula Rubra' (Weeping Spring Cherry)

Pyrus salicifolia 'Pendula' (Weeping Pear)

Rhus trichocarpa (Sumach)

Salix matsudana 'Tortuosa' (Corkscrew Willow)

Sorbus hostii (Mountain Ash)

Turn those junk CDs into bird scarers in a flash!

Have you had a good look at your junk mail recently? You will probably find that you are throwing out countless promotional CDs, which make excellent bird scarers! When hung over seed beds, fruit bushes and in fruit trees the wary birds are deterred when the reflective surfaces of the CDs give sudden flashes of light. The birds won't disappear from your garden completely – just from the areas that you choose.

Don't get in a flap over floppy tulips!

It has happened to everyone I am sure. A vase of tulips looks wonderful for a few hours then the heads start to droop. Don't despair because help is at hand from an unusual source – a pin. All that is required is for you to carefully push a pin in and out, right through the stem of the tulip just where it joins the head of the bloom. Then wait. After half an hour or so the tulip head should rise up again! Before you apply to join The Magic Circle let me explain the secret of the 'trick'. When you fill a vase with water from the tap you are dragging bubbles of air into the water. Tulip stems are hollow and where the stem meets the flower head it narrows a little and air bubbles get trapped, preventing water from reaching the bloom. Using the pin simply releases the trapped air.

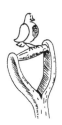

Roll on the weedkiller with your homemade spot weeder!

The gardening industry loves you to spend money and tempts you with products that frankly are an unnecessary expense. Take the 'spot weeder' for the lawn. This is simply ordinary lawn weedkiller in a fancy applicator. Don't buy one; make your own using an empty roll-on deodorant container. Just prise off the ball, wash out well and fill, carefully, with ordinary lawn weedkiller diluted as per the bottle. Push the ball back on and, hey presto, you have your own roll-on weedkiller for use on that odd lawn weed or when it is too windy to spray the lawn. Oh, yes, do me a favour – label it!

Cut off those telltale onion tips

Prevent birds from pulling onion sets out of the ground by simply cutting off the dead tips of the sets before planting. It is those that the birds look for. The birds won't easily spot them and should leave your onions alone.

Floppy perennials need the basket treatment

A wire hanging basket placed upside down over emerging, tall-stemmed perennials makes a great support for the stems as they grow. No more unsightly canes to poke you in the eye!

A watering pot makes a difference to thirsty plants

If you grow plants, such as sunflowers, which require a good supply of water, then sink a 5" plastic flowerpot alongside the plant at planting time. You can then water into the pot and be confident that the majority of the water is going straight where it is needed – to the roots.

Steve's top 20 rabbit-proof perennials . . .

Agapanthus 'Blue Giant' (African Lily)

Aconitum 'Blue Sceptre' (Monskshood)

Alchemilla mollis (Lady's Mantle)

Anemone x hybrida (Windflower)

Aquilegia vulgaris (Columbine)

Aster novi-belgi (Michaelmas Daisy)

Bergenia species (Elephant's Ears)

Convallaria majalis (Lily of the Valley)

Crocosmia 'Lucifer' (Montbretia)

Digitalis pupurea (Foxglove)

Euphorbia griffithii 'Fireglow' (Spurge)

Helleborus hybridus (Lenten Rose)

Kniphofia triangularis (Red Hot Poker)

Lamium maculatum 'Beacon Silver' (Dead Nettle)

Narcissus species (Daffodil)

Nepeta faassenii (Catmint)

Paeonia officianalis (Peony)

Pulmonaria saccharata (Jerusalem Sage)

Sedum telephium 'Matrona' (Ice Plant)

Trollius x cultorum (Globeflower)

Steve's top 20 rabbit-proof shrubs . . .

Arundinaria species (Bamboo)

Buxus sempervirens (Box)

Ceanothus thyrisiflorus var. repens

Cornus sanguinea 'Winter Beauty' (Common Dogwood)

Cotoneaster horizontalis

Fuchsia species

Gaultheria mucronata 'Mulberry Wine' (Pernettya)

Hypericum calycinum (Rose of Sharon)

Kalmia latifolia (Calico Bush)

Laurus nobilis (Bay)

Lonicera species (Honeysuckle)

Prunus laurocerasus (Cherry Laurel)

Rhododendron species

Rosa 'Rosy Cushion' (Shrub Rose)

Rosmarinus officinalis (Rosemary)

Ruscus aculeatus (Butcher's Broom)

Sambucus nigra (Golden Elder)

Skimmia japonica

Spirea japonica 'Anthony Waterer'

Vinca species (Periwinkle)

Ferret droppings make moles run a mile

There are few garden pests that cause more devastation to a well-kept lawn or border than the unassuming mole. I say unassuming because the little fellow is only a few inches in length and really doesn't mean to cause you stress. He is just going about his normal daily business, which includes digging up your lawn, and leaving hills of freshly moved soil! Don't even consider killing him. That is barbaric. Instead use a natural approach. The smell of the dung of a predator is usually more than enough to scare off most animals.

The natural predator of the mole is the badger but it is notoriously difficult to get badger poo! Luckily a close relative of the badger is the ferret and poor old Mr Mole can't tell the difference. It is somewhat easier to obtain ferret droppings, as members of local ferret associations are only too happy to part with the stuff! Once obtained, mix with a little water to make a paste, dig out the mole hill until you find the run and paint the ferret-poo paste around the rim of the entrance, or put a mound just inside. The wind will take the smell of the ferret down the hole, the mole will get a whiff, think "badger!" and scarper quick – never to darken your garden gate again!

The garden cure for traveller's tummy!

This is not exactly a gardening tip, more advice on a couple of useful plants to grow – lemon verbena and angelica. Sprigs of these two aromatic herbs make wonderful cures for travel sickness. Place under the feet of the susceptible passenger and tell them to periodically tread on them. This will release the aroma, which will quickly alleviate nausea as well as making the car smell fresh.

Filter your water with a pair of tights

Rainwater in a water butt can easily go sour if leaves that get into it are allowed to rot down. The simplest way of avoiding this is to cover the end of the water down pipe that feeds into the water butt with a stocking or leg of a pair of tights. This acts as a filter and collects the offending leaves. You must remember, though, to regularly clean out your homemade filter.

Paraffin protection from munching mice!

Mice, you will find, are particularly fond of newly planted pea and bean seeds. Mice on the other hand are not that turned on by the smell of paraffin! Solution? Soak your pea and bean seeds in paraffin before sowing. The seed coat absorbs enough paraffin to keep the rodents away until the seeds have safely germinated. If you find mice are also pinching your spring flowering bulbs then soak the bulbs in a solution of 1 tablespoon of paraffin to 1 pint of water and this should keep them safe.

Make a note of this tip!

Always get into the habit of taking a small notebook and sharpened pencil whenever you go visiting gardens. You can then easily jot down all the must-have plants you discover and new planting ideas that come to mind. It's amazing how much you forget when you get back home!

There's something fishy on the compost heap!

Now here's a thought - goldfish are good for the garden! Well not the fish itself, but the goldfish bowl water, often sent down the plug hole at changing time should actually be sent down the garden to the compost heap where its rich nutrient composition can really work wonders.

Steve's top herbs for a summer hanging basket . . .

Basil – try lemon, lime, Thai and sweet green varieties (not hardy)
Chervil
Chives
Coriander (not hardy)
Dill - fern-leaf variety
Garlic chives
Lemon Balm
Mint - try apple, pineapple or ginger varieties
Nasturtiums (not strictly a herb but great edible leaves and flowers!)
Oregano
Parsley – flat leaved varieties have more flavour
Rosemary (in centre – move when too large)
Sage - variegated
Tarragon
Thyme – try common and lemon varieties

The basket will need at least 4 hours of sun each day - more if possible. Try to shelter the basket from the wind, or at least move it on very windy days. Use good, free-draining compost and if you are using herbs like mint or basil, you'll want a pretty fertile mixture so mix in some slow release fertilizer. The Mediterranean herbs such as rosemary, thyme or sage need a little sand added for extra drainage.

Brush your pond clean of annoying blanket weed

Blanket weed in a pond can be a nightmare to remove and you can spend hours trying to scoop it out. The quick and easy solution is to buy a cheap, round hairbrush and tie this firmly to a long pole or bamboo cane. Push the hairbrush into the weed and twist round and round. The weed neatly wraps itself around the brush allowing you to remove it completely.

Even rabbits can have a use in the garden!

The straw from the weekly changes of the guinea pig or rabbit hutch can go straight into the bottom of the prepared trenches for legumes (i.e. peas and beans). A 2" layer of the straw, together with all the droppings will give that nitrogen rich boost to the plants, as well as helping to conserve water in the soil.

The gloves are on for these troublesome weeds

Some weeds are just impossible to get rid of without a bit of chemical help unless you are able to take away areas of soil so the whole root system can be removed. Bindweed, mare's-tail and ground elder fall into this category. Breaking them off at the soil surface exacerbates the problem as the roots just produce many more plants. Control requires the use of a glyphosate-based herbicide. Glyphosate works systemically by travelling through the plant to kill the root. When in contact with the soil it is rendered harmless. These attributes make glyphosate the most environmentally friendly of the weed killers available. The trouble is that it will kill any green plant that it comes in contact with which makes using it in between other plants a challenge.

The answer is quite simple. First make up a solution of glyphosate-based weed killer in a bucket. Then put on a new rubber glove followed by an old woollen glove or sock over the top. Dip this hand into the solution and squeeze out any excess liquid. Now carefully reach through your plants, take hold of the offending weed, and let it run through your gloved hand. Enough weed killer will be on the weed for the glyphosate to take effect without harming your other plants. To deal really effectively with bindweed, as soon as you notice it place a short bamboo cane in the soil next to the plant and train it up the cane over the following weeks. Then your gloved weed-killing job is made much easier.

Longer lasting fence posts

A fence post will last a lot longer in the ground before it rots if you soak the bottom 18" in old engine oil for a few days, then wrap the end in cling film before concreting in the ground. A bit of effort, I agree, but you have added a few years to the life of the post!

Laddered tights give loads of ties!

Old laddered pairs of tights or stockings can be cut into strips to make useful ties for gentle climbers such as clematis as well as staked perennials. The stretching nature of the material allows for movement in the wind.

Bubble-wrap your plants for great winter insulation

Bubble-wrap may be brilliant for protecting your valuables in the post but don't be too quick to dispose of even the smallest bits. It makes excellent insulation for the greenhouse allowing you to save heating costs and raise earlier flower and veg plants. Wrapped around your patio pots and over the soil surface it may look a bit odd, but will give frost protection for the roots of less hardy shrubs and perennials.

Homemade winter bird feeder

Feeding the birds is a very rewarding hobby and, in order to get those that don't migrate to stay in your garden all year, you must switch the food in autumn to one with a high fat content. This will help the birds build up a good layer of fatty tissue to survive the winter. Making your own high fat feeder is easy, fun, and the birds will love it! Melt 8oz of lard in a pan and mix in a tablespoon each of porridge oats, wild birdseed, chopped peanuts and dried fruit. Before the mixture sets pour into empty yoghurt pots with a length of string dangled in the middle. Leave the pots in the fridge to set then tip out your bird's banquet and hang outside by the string.

(DON'T FORGET TO TAKE THE FOOD OUT OF THE POTS!)

Longer-lasting labels

Even if you use a permanent marker pen on your plant labels, the ink still seems to fade. To stop this happening, as soon as you have written on the label give the writing a quick covering of clear nail varnish and the ink will last much longer. This also means that you don't have to hunt for a waterproof marker – any one will do!

Ready salted cabbages?

Avoid the devastating effect of caterpillars munching through the leaves of your brassicas by watering the young plants with a dilute table salt solution. One tablespoon to two gallons of water will be sufficient. The salt is taken into the plant leaves making them unpalatable for caterpillars. As the plants mature, the salt will be lost from the leaves so the edible brassicas won't be tainted.

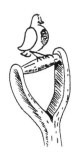

Grated soap puts even the hungriest squirrel off its dinner

A gardener's life can easily turn into a running battle with the squirrel. Cute when they are performing their acrobatics atop your fence or in a tree but not so cute when they are doing the same with a fat, juicy crocus bulb in their mouth! Accept the fact that you will have to live with nature's prettiest rodent and leave some over ripe apples as a sign of your offer of truce. Then protect all your planted bulbs with the best squirrel deterrent there is – grated soap! The cheaper and more smelly the better. Squirrels hate the smell of it and will avoid it like the plague. Simply grate up the soap and sprinkle over the surface of the soil or compost where you have planted any bulbs. You may have to re-apply after rain but a bar of soap is cheap enough and should last you all season.

Roofing felt repels slugs and snails

Slugs and snails feature a lot in this book! Squares of green mineral roofing felt – the type on your garden shed roof – is a great way of ensuring that the slimy pests can't reach your plants. Cut a hole in the middle of a 6" square of the felt, wide enough to fit around the plant stem. Now cut a slit halfway across to enable you to slip the square, like a collar, around the plant. There are two reasons why slugs and snails are loathed to traverse the felt. Firstly the surface is very rough which hurts their underbellies, and secondly, they appear to hate the smell of the bitumen glue in the felt, especially on a warm summer's evening.

Bananas make roses grow out of their skins

Roses are probably the hungriest plants in your garden and when coming into flower they are looking for one particular plant food – potassium. Proprietary rose feeds contain this, as does the generic sulphate of potash, but for that added boost of potassium look no further than your fruit bowl for the humble banana. The middle bit may be good for us but the best bit for your roses is the skin – it is full of potassium! Chop up banana skins into small pieces and fork them into the surface of the soil at the base of the rose bush. As they quickly rot down they will release their potassium into the soil in a form that the rose can use immediately – no waiting until it is mixed with other chemicals in the soil. The result is better flowering roses with larger, longer-lasting blooms, stronger scents, richer colours and bigger, brighter hips. What more could you want?

Give tiny seeds a perfect start with a toothpaste tube

Sowing very tiny seeds can be a difficult task. You need to be able to spread them thinly and not lose them first. This can be achieved easily with nothing more than an empty toothpaste tube and a packet of non-fungicidal wallpaper paste. First cut the bottom off the toothpaste tube and clean out well with warm water. Next, in a small bowl and depending on how many seeds you have to sow, mix two or three tablespoons of the wallpaper paste to a gel according to the instructions. Sprinkle your tiny seeds into the gel and mix very quickly. Amazingly, the wonder of physics spaces the seeds like atoms, equidistant to each other in the gel. Now carefully spoon the gel into the toothpaste tube. Take your prepared seed tray of compost and roll down the tube from the bottom, whilst squeezing the gel into a drill in the surface. Finally cover the gel if necessary, with a thin layer of compost. Some seeds will not need covering as they need light to germinate. Your seeds are now not only evenly spread but also have a water reservoir in the gel and some extra food when the cellulose of the wallpaper paste eventually breaks down.

Steve's top 20 plants for an autumn leaf firework display . . .

Acer palmatum 'Senkaki'

Acer palmatum 'Osakazuki'

Aronia arbutifolia 'Erecta' (Chokeberry)

Amelanchier lamarkii (Snowy Mespilus)

Berberis x media 'Red Jewel' (Barberry)

Callicarpa japonica (Beauty Berry)

Cornus alba 'Kesselringii' (Red-barked Dogwood)

Cornus alba 'Sibirica' (another Red-barked Dogwood!)

Cornus sanguinea 'Winter Flame' (Common Dogwood)

Cotinus 'Flame' (Smoke Bush)

Euonymus europaeus 'Red Cascade' (Spindleberry)

Fothergilla gardenia (needs acid soil)

Hamamelis x intermedia 'Feuerzauber'

Hydrangea quercifolia (Oak-leaved Hydrangea - great in a tub)

Oxydendrum arboreum (Sorrel Tree - needs acid soil)

Parthenocissus tricuspidata (Boston Ivy)

Prunus incisa 'Kojo-no-mai' (Fuji Cherry)

Ribes odoratum (Buffalo Currant)

Spirea betulifolia var. aemelina

Vaccinium corymbosum (Highbush Blueberry)

Building supplies for the birds

Finding good nesting material can be a real headache for birds in late winter and early spring. You can help them by filling a piece of netting with all manner of useful nest building materials and hanging outside so that the birds can easily pull bits through the net and use it like a haberdashery. Materials that birds find really useful include: straw, shredded paper, strands of wool & cotton, animal or human hair & thin twigs. One of the best things I have found, which House Martins in particular seem to like, is the shredded wheat type breakfast cereal! They don't eat it – they wet it with saliva and use it as a mortar for 'plastering' their nests giving them a modern 'oatmeal' look. It could catch on! Along with all this construction assistance, feed the birds regularly and they will become frequent visitors to your garden.

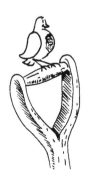

Cute cane top covers

The garden can be a dangerous place for your eyes if you have bamboo canes around supporting your plants. There are many things that you can put atop a cane to make it safer but I think one of the best is a rubber teat from a baby's bottle! Make friends with someone with a new addition to the family and scrounge their old teats – they fit perfectly onto a cane!

Garlic is a real turn off for broad bean blackfly

Garlic has some wonderful culinary and medicinal uses for us and your garden can benefit as well. A few cloves planted in between rows of broad beans will deter blackfly – the vampire pests of broad bean plants, sucking the sap out of the succulent new shoots. You won't smell the garlic unless the leaves are crushed but the nasally superior blackfly will get a whiff and depart!

Never leave home without your 'cuttings kit'!

Don't get the wrong idea with this tip. You have to ask permission first! Whenever you are out visiting friends' gardens or on a country walk always have a 'cuttings kit' in your pocket. This indispensable item consists of two or three small plastic sandwich bags, a few short lengths of garden twine, a few sheets of very damp kitchen paper and a small sharp penknife. Armed thus you will always be prepared should you spot a 'must-have' cutting or two. Wrap the end of the cutting in a sheet of damp tissue, pop into a plastic bag, tie the top with a piece of twine and the plant material should survive until you get back home where you can properly deal with its planting.

Steve's calendar for a lovely lawn

March
As soon as the grass begins to grow and the conditions are right, gently rake the lawn to remove leaves and surface rubbish. The first cut should be just to remove the top $1/2$" of the grass. Close cutting now will result in severe yellowing. If moss is a real problem, apply a liquid moss killer now, and rake out the black, dead moss two weeks later.

April
Busy month! Mow often enough to stop the grass growing too long, but do not cut lower than about $1^1/2$". Don't mow if the grass is wet or frosted. Always brush off any debris such as leaves, twigs and especially worm casts, with a besom broom if available. Feeding and weeding can begin towards the end of the month as long as the grass and the weeds are actively growing, so have a careful inspection. This is a good time for sowing a new lawn as grass seed germinates quicker with the changes in temperature in spring.

May
Increase the frequency of mowing as necessary and lower the height of cut to about 1". Usually weekly mowing can begin. If feeding and weeding was not carried out last month then do it as soon as possible before things get serious! Water the lawn if a prolonged dry spell occurs: don't wait for the grass to go yellow. Regularly check over the lawn for any signs of problems.

June
Summer mowing should be underway by now, cutting twice a week if possible to keep the grass to about 1". If a dry spell occurs then reduce mowing and raise the cutting height.

Giving the lawn a light raking before mowing will help keep clover runners under control. This is the time for summer lawn feeding, using a high nitrogen product. Carefully examine the turf: if weeds are a problem then treat as for April. If hot weather has baked the soil surface, then prick the lawn with a sharp fork before watering or feeding and weeding.

July
Mow regularly at the summer height; water if the weather is dry; rake as for June; spot weed any persistent weeds that appear. If you are on holiday for a fortnight or more then make arrangements for mowing and watering in your absence, otherwise you could undo all your efforts of the past months!

August
Same general treatment as for July. August is the last month for you to carry out any weed killing or feeding with a nitrogen-rich tonic. If you return from holiday to long grass then raise the cutting height on the mower for the first cut. If you return from holiday to dead grass then keep the bottle of Ouzo you bought to thank your neighbour for looking after your lawn, and drink it yourself! Happy mowing!

September

Increase the interval between mowing and raise the cutting height to $1^1/_2$". This allows the grass to grow a little higher, and will help to reduce the chance of frost penetrating the turf and damaging it. Get rid of the moss first, using a moss killer. Two weeks later you can scarify the lawn to remove the dead moss. Moss is often a sign of poor growing conditions, such as bad drainage, excessive shade, compaction, low fertility and over-acidity. To tackle poor drainage and compaction, aerate the lawn and apply a top dressing (see October). To improve fertility, feed the lawn. To remove shade, prune back overhanging trees and shrubs. To reduce acidity, apply lime - such as ground chalk or ground limestone - at no more than $1^1/_2$oz per sq yd.

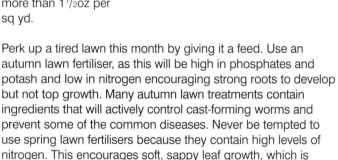

Perk up a tired lawn this month by giving it a feed. Use an autumn lawn fertiliser, as this will be high in phosphates and potash and low in nitrogen encouraging strong roots to develop but not top growth. Many autumn lawn treatments contain ingredients that will actively control cast-forming worms and prevent some of the common diseases. Never be tempted to use spring lawn fertilisers because they contain high levels of nitrogen. This encourages soft, sappy leaf growth, which is vulnerable to disease.

September is a good month to carry out any lawn repairs with turf or seed, as the soil is warm and moist.

October

Scarify the lawn this month. This means vigorously raking the lawn to remove the layer of old grass clippings, moss and other rubbish that builds up in the turf, encouraging disease. Getting rid of this will allow water and fertilisers to reach the grass roots more easily and in turn will improve grass growth. Scarifying also stimulates the grass to produce side shoots and runners. You can use a spring-tine rake, or hire or buy an electric scarifier. Improve the drainage on compacted areas of the lawn by aerating it with a garden fork or hollow-tine tool. Once you've aerated the soil, late October it is a good time to apply a top dressing. A simple mixture of three parts of loam, six parts of sharp sand and one part of peat substitute will suit most soils. Apply at about 4lb per sq yd and brush it into the lawn surface.

Regular mowing comes to an end during October. For the last cut or two raise the cutter height a fraction and make sure that you brush off any raindrops or dew before cutting. Rake up any fallen leaves.

November

If we have an extended autumn you may wish to mow the grass with the blades set high. Clean all equipment and book the mower in for a winter service. Coat the blades with a little cooking oil to ensure they do not develop any rust.

December / January

Apart from brushing away any leaves, these months offer a slack time to a busy year on the lawn. Keep off the grass if it is frozen or very wet.

February

Watch out for worm casts from new worms, brush them off as necessary and await the appearance of a wonderful lawn in March!

Soluble aspirin is just what the doctor ordered for stunted plants

Do you have a plant suffering from stunted growth? Does the label say 8' but you've only got 8"? Your plant is probably short of growth hormone and has lost the ability to make any more for itself.

Without realising it, in your medicine cabinet you probably have some plant growth hormone, except it is labelled 'soluble aspirin'! This is almost identical to the naturally occurring growth hormone in plants and they can't tell the difference. One soluble aspirin in a pint of water every couple of weeks will kick the plant back into growth and it can start making more hormone for itself.

A juicy solution to dog dead grass!

Nothing will kill grass faster than dog urine, especially that of the bitch dog. No matter how fast you are with a bucket of water to dilute the offending dog wee it still seems to be strong enough to produce those telltale dead patches. Extra feeding of the grass also has little effect. Well, forget the lawn itself, because the answer lies with the dog and a bottle of tomato juice. Twice a day mix 1½ tablespoons of tomato juice with the dog's food – once in the morning, once in the evening. The reason for the timing is all to do with the working of the dog's bladder. Amazingly the tomato juice neutralises the chemical in the dog's urine that kills the grass. The dog can then wee all over the lawn with no ill effects to the grass. Unfortunately you have to keep up the dosage of juice every single day to maintain the effect!

Steve's 20 summer stunners . . .

Euphorbia griffithii 'Dixter' (Spurge)

Anemone rivularus (Windflower)

Rosa 'Louise Odier' (Bourbon rose)

Clematis 'Bees' Jubilee'

Clematis 'The President'

Rosa 'Souvenir du Docteur Jamain'

Lonicera x tellmanniana (Honeysuckle)

Passiflora caerulea (Passion Flower)

Eremurus x isabellinus 'Cleopatra' (Foxtail Lily)

Allium flavum, Allium 'Globemaster' and *Allium karataviense* (Ornamental Onions)

Philadelphus 'Belle Etoile' (Mock Orange)

Lavendua stoechas (French lavender)

Sidalcea 'Elsie Heugh' (False Mallow)

Papaver rhoeas 'Mother of Pearl' (Poppy)

Catananche caerulea (Cupid's Dart)

Eryngium x zabelii, Eryngium variifolium and *Eryngium alpinum* (Sea Holly)

Penstemon 'Stapleford Blue'

Phlox paniculata 'Barnwell'

Scabiosa caucasica 'Clive Greaves' (Scabious)

Lobelia 'Bee's Flame'

Sugar water keeps your Christmas tree fully clothed

A Christmas tree devoid of needles can be a common sight in our modern centrally heated rooms. The dry air causes the needles to drop despite your best efforts of keeping it standing in water. You can buy sprays for the leaves, which are reputed to help, but a good way of reducing needle drop is to keep your water reservoir topped up with sugar water. A 1lb bag of sugar dissolved in 2 gallons of water will do the trick. The sugar is taken into the plant system and helps to keep the needles attached.

Horsehair gives slugs and snails stomach ache!

Natural looking slug and snail deterrents are the best, and horsehair looks the part and works a treat. Stables get rid of huge quantities every week so you can easily scrounge some. Place it in a 4" diameter ring around susceptible plants and weight down with stones. Make sure, though, that the stones don't form a bridge for the slimy pests! Slugs and snails cannot crawl over the hair for two reasons – the hair is an irritant and the grease in it reacts with their slime and burns their underbellies. Have you ever seen a horse covered in snails? Well there you are then!

Hanging baskets need a good soaking

A quick and easy way to give a hanging basket a good soaking, after planting, is to hang it from a broom handle across the open top of a water butt or stand the basket on a large bucket of water. Only the bottom inch of the basket needs to be in the water for capillary action to water the whole basket. Usually about an hour is needed for the whole basket to become soaked. This is also a good tip to use should the basket get very dry at times during the summer, when normal watering from above just seems to run off the dry compost.

There's no better bird feeder than nature's own cone

When you pick up a large pinecone with the open bracts that have released all their seeds, what you unknowingly have in your hands is nature's custom made bird feeder! The bracts are springy and will hold all kinds of tasty treats for the birds – nuts, fat, bread, cheese, stale cake or biscuits, bacon rind, boiled potato – whatever suitable scraps you can find. Once filled you can easily hang it up with string tied around the top bracts or through a hole drilled in the top. At Christmastime, before filling with food, spray the cones with gold or silver paint for a really festive look!

Be prepared for those new arrivals

You never know when you will need to plant up a cutting. It may be one that you have been given by a generous gardening friend or perhaps you have brought some back from a visit to a friend's garden. It is a good idea to always have a tray of prepared cutting compost ready in the shed or greenhouse so you can pot up that potential new plant without delay. A mix of two parts ordinary multi-purpose compost to one part sharp sand and one part horticultural grit is ideal as it gives the excellent drainage required for rooting. When the plant is growing strongly it can be moved to a more compost rich medium.

A wall of food – every climbing plant's dream!

Climbing plants planted at the base of a wall can often struggle to find the necessary food as they grow. A good tip is to actually pre-spray the wall with a liquid foliar feed before planting. As the plant grows it will obtain nourishment from the wall's surface and put on much faster growth. Repeat the application every few weeks and the plant should never go hungry.

Defensive rings against the slugs and snails

Cut into 3" diameter rings, empty plastic pop bottles make great slug and snail guards for your small susceptible plants. The sharp plastic edge is usually enough to stop them. Carefully push the rings over the plants and about an inch into the soil. Then fill them with an extra deterrent such as sharp grit or broken eggshells.

Mirrors give carrot root fly a real headache!

This is one of those unbelievable but true tips! Carrot root fly can devastate a crop and you can be oblivious to it until you start to pull the roots and see the damage that the larvae have done. But there is hope and it's all to do with finding out all about the enemy. The female carrot root fly is the problem. She flies along the row of carrots at a height of about $1^1/_2$ " above the soil with a territory length of just over a yard. Before she lays her eggs, she will ensure that other carrot root flies do not infiltrate her patch, by flying up and down viciously attacking any that she sees. That is her Achilles heel! By standing old handbag mirrors back to back at one-yard intervals along the row of carrots, the female carrot root fly will, amazingly, attack her reflection and keep up the attack until she drops dead at the base of the mirror. Neat trick eh?!

Steve's top 20 plants for walls and fences . . .

Ampelopsis brevipendunculata

Buddleia alternifolia (Butterfly Bush)

Ceanothus impressus

Clematis armandii 'Apple Blossom'

Clematis cirrhosa balearica 'Freckles'

Clematis orientalis 'Bill McKenzie'

Chaenomeles x superba 'Crimson & Gold' (Ornamental Quince)

Cytisus battandieri (Pineapple Broom)

Hedera colchica 'Sulphur Heart' (Ivy)

Hydrangea petiolaris (Climbing Hydrangea)

Jasminum beesianum (Summer Jasmine)

Kolkwitzia amabilis (Beauty Bush)

Lonicera x brownii 'Dropmore Scarlet' (Honeysuckle)

Lonicera periclymenum 'Sweet Sue' (Honeysuckle)

Parthenocissus henryana (variegated Virginia Creeper)

Passiflora caerulea (Passion Flower)

Philadelphus burkwoodii (Mock Orange)

Rosa 'Mme Alfred Carriere' (Climbing Rose)

Rosa 'New Dawn, Climbing' (Climbing Rose)

Rosa 'Warm Welcome' (Climbing Rose)

Tease out those weeds with a pair of tweezers

Weeding in between delicate seedlings and around the base of fragile potted plants can be a tricky job. Using a pair of eyebrow tweezers makes the job a whole lot easier! After use, however, remember to return the tweezers to whoever lent them to you.

Beer makes your houseplant leaves breathe more easily!

Houseplants can often be the most neglected plants, especially when the seasonal emphasis is on the garden outside. Foliage houseplants in particular suffer because the pores of their leaves get blocked – not just with dust but also with bacteria. Cleaning the leaves with leaf wipes may make them shine but it does nothing to kill the bacteria. In order to grow healthily, a plant's leaves must breathe through their pores and exchange gases. Blocked pores means the plant could choke to death. Help is at hand with the best anti-bacterial cleaner for plant leaves – beer! The weak acid in beer will successfully kill the harmful bacteria in the pores. A weekly clean of both sides of the leaves with cotton wool soaked in beer will do the trick.

Shock snails into submission with a bit of copper wire!

Snails are the mountaineers of the garden and boy can they climb! If 30ft up a laburnum tree is no big deal for them then a couple of feet up the side of your hosta pot is an evening stroll to a living McDonalds! Elsewhere in this tome of terrific tips are other ideas to keep slugs and snails away from your plants but this tip is shocking – literally! Read on . . .

Take two thin strands of copper wire. Used bell cable with the plastic coating stripped off will work just fine. Tightly tie the wires around the pot, approximately $1/2$" apart. There must be no gaps for the little devils to squeeze under! Then, in the evening, go and find yourself a snail. Place the snail on the pot and watch it climb. When it crawls over the first copper wire - no problem. Then, with its bum on the first wire its front end will touch the second wire. Immediately a small electric current is set up by the reaction between the snail slime and the copper and the snail gets a shock and falls off the pot! Hilarious fun for all the family!

Growing your own mini-turves is easy

When you have small dead patches of grass to repair on your lawn the easiest solution is to grow your own mini-turves. Line a half or full sized seed tray with about 6 layers of absorbent kitchen paper and moisten well. Sow your grass seed thickly over the surface and press the seed into the wet paper. Place the trays on a well-lit windowsill, keep moist and turn regularly. After a couple of weeks you will have a mini-turf growing through the kitchen paper. When the grass is about $1/2$ " high you can lift out the 'turf', cut to size with scissors and set in the prepared spot on the lawn. Growing it in this way you have avoided loss of seedlings to the birds, established a good root system and provided a moisture retentive medium for the first few months. And you feel clever!

Why pick a whole cucumber when half will do?

How many times have you picked a whole cucumber from the greenhouse and had to throw half of it away a week or so later when it has gone soft? Next time just cut half a cucumber from the plant and cover the end of the remaining half with cling film held in place with a rubber band. It will stay fresh on the plant a lot longer than in the fridge!

Immovable orchids for irresistible flowers

If you want longer lasting orchid flowers then it is vital not to move the plant at all when it is in flower. Even a slight turn of the pot can cause the flower stalks to twist and the blooms to drop off. Left alone an orchid can hold its flowers for months.

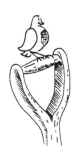

Cutting remarks!

If you find it difficult to get cuttings of particular plants to root, then use a much simpler approach. Take a couple of cuttings from these plants every month from spring until late autumn. The plant won't mind and you are sure to have success on some occasions. Also don't be too heavy handed with the hormone rooting powder! As a rule of thumb, if you can easily see the powder on the end of the cutting you have used too much. A tiny speck is all that is needed to trick the end of the stem into producing roots. Finally, never use the rooting powder on pelargoniums or other fleshy plant cuttings. These will root quite happily without help and the powder can actually clog up the stem and cause it to rot.

Barley straw for a crystal clear pond

Green, algae-infested water in your pond is not an attractive sight. There is no need to try an array of chemicals to solve the problem; all you need is some barley straw. Small, handy-sized bales are available from many garden centres or you can make your own with some barley straw and some plastic garden netting. Just toss the bale into the pond and let nature do the work. A chemical given off by the barley straw in the water will kill off the algae while causing no harm to fish or other wildlife.

An empty egg box makes a super seed collector

An empty egg box makes an ideal collecting container for the many sorts of free seeds that nature gives the patient gardener from late summer. Always leave a few dead flower stems to give you these seeds and carefully tap them in to the egg box compartments, labelling each one accordingly. Back inside, carefully cut out the compartments and transfer each lot of seeds into individual envelopes marked with the details of the plant and date of collection. Store the envelope in a used ice cream container in the fridge until sowing time the following spring.

Bottomless pots give grow bag success

Growing tomatoes in a grow bag is certainly a space saving way but you can increase yield and make staking, watering and feeding easier with a simple adaptation at planting time. Instead of planting the tomato plants directly into the grow bag, plant them into 7" diameter bottomless plastic flowerpots pushed about 1" deep into the revealed compost of the grow bag. The plants get established quicker in the added depth of compost before competing with the roots of the other plants in the main part of the grow bag.

Cooling grass seed really hots up the germination!

You may have noticed how reluctant grass seed is to germinate in the warmth of summer but seems to do it much faster in spring and autumn? This is no reflection on the quality of the seed or your expert preparation of the area to be seeded, it's all to do with a peculiar fact about grass seed. It germinates, not because of the actual temperature but due to a sudden change in temperature – the sort of condition that you find more readily in spring and autumn. Summer sown grass seed can be tricked into germinating quickly by keeping it in the freezer for a couple of days prior to planting. The sudden change in temperature from the cold freezer to the warm soil is all that is required!

Cocktail sticks ensure that kitty's not sitting pretty on your tubs!

Cats can be easily persuaded to avoid using your newly planted seed trays, containers and window boxes as convenient loo stops by peppering the surface of the compost with cocktail sticks, leaving about $3/4$" protruding. Listen out - the cat will only try it one more time!

Seal in the water before summer moving

Moving shrubs in the middle of summer can be a dangerous thing. Often, until they become re-established, they will lose more water through their leaves than they can replace from the soil, and the resulting dying plant is an all too common sight. If you really have to move a shrub at this time, protection from desiccation can easily be achieved by spraying the whole plant an hour or so before with a non-fungicidal cellulose wallpaper paste, ensuring that both sides of the leaves are covered. This prevents water loss from the leaves. After a few days of recovery the paste can then be hosed off the plant.

Style your hanging baskets with old jumpers

Next time you have a clear out of your wardrobe, keep any dark coloured woolly jumpers or fleeces you intend to throw out as they make great linings for hanging baskets. You can easily cut out planting holes and they are big enough to fit any size of basket.

Make a lacewing and ladybird log cabin

For a natural balance in your garden you need to attract beneficial insects to help keep the pests under control. A bundle of 6" lengths of hollowed out bamboo canes provides a brilliant home for over wintering lacewings and ladybirds – two of the most useful predators of aphids.

Epsom Salts – the perfect plant pick-me-up!

Many plants in containers, particularly houseplants, can suffer from magnesium deficiency – recognisable by a browning of the leaves between the veins. Trace element feeds can rectify the problem but once again you could probably have saved money by taking a look in the bathroom cabinet. Epsom salts (magnesium sulphate) is the perfect way to revitalise those plants that are short of magnesium. One teaspoon of the salts to a pint of water every couple of weeks and the plant is back on its feet.

Homemade compost scoop saves time & mess

Using a trowel to get compost out of one of the large bags can be a frustrating experience! Just as you reach the lip of the bag it bends in and knocks most of the compost off the trowel. You can avoid this by making your own compost scoop very simply from one of the large plastic pop bottles with a built-in handle. Cut the bottle at an angle about 8" along from the cap end, making sure that the handle is in line with the angled cut. This scoop will hold about three times the amount of a trowel. Oh yes, remember to keep the top on the bottle!

Fast food containers for fast germination

If you want to germinate small quantities of seeds and don't want the windowsill cluttered with seed trays then, instead, use the polystyrene hinged burger boxes from the fast food joints – they are perfect. All you need to do is to make some holes in the base with a hot knitting needle for drainage. The polystyrene gives great insulation and germination is speeded up. Be sure to leave the lid open as soon as the seedlings appear. Drip trays for your 'mini-propagators' can be easily made by cutting another burger box in half.

Tea leaves make a super iron feed for plants

Never throw away used tea bags. They can be used to make a great iron rich feed for your plants, particularly acid loving ones. Keep a jug of water on the kitchen work surface and drop the spent tea bags into it. At the end of the week simply pour the liquid directly around your plants and put the bags on the compost heap where they will rot down. The liquid feed also provides a much needed iron-rich top up for houseplants. If you don't fancy making the liquid feed then just break the tea bags open and mulch them into the soil at the base of your plants.

Bed and breakfast for the butterflies

Stinging nettles and thistles may not be the first plants on your list for a beautiful garden but they should be if you want to encourage butterflies to assist in the pollination of your plants. Pollination gives you free seeds from the flower bed and plentiful crops of beans, cucumbers, tomatoes etc... on the vegetable plot. Butterflies will not feed on the same plants as they breed on, so as well as having lots of buddleias, scabious, sedums and other butterfly feeding stations, make sure you provide them with a bed or they will go elsewhere to lay their eggs. Stinging nettles and thistles offer the butterflies protection for their newly emerged caterpillars, so keep a small, managed patch of these plants in the bottom corner of the garden.

An early spray for roses does the trick

Roses are lovely flowers but the plants are often susceptible to blackspot. Obviously you want to avoid excessive spraying all through the season so you diligently follow the spray manufacturer's instructions and spray as soon as the leaf buds break. Let me tell you a secret – you are about a week too late! You can reduce the amount of times that you need to spray roses against blackspot by spraying the plant when the buds swell but before they break, ensuring that the spray gets into the stem joints, to kill any over-wintering disease spores. Also spray the soil around the rose bush to a diameter of about 12", again to kill any spores. If you fail to spray the soil, any blackspot spores will be bounced up onto the plant during the first heavy spring show of rain.

Say goodbye to holey hostas

Problem: it seems that whatever slug and snail protection you put around the hostas growing in your flower border, they still get decimated. Well firstly, the slug and snail barrier that you are using, be it broken egg shells, grit, soot etc.., is working just fine. The problem will have started in the previous autumn. This was when your old hosta leaves were dying off and, being a good gardener, you left the leaves to go completely brown so that all the goodness could return to the root stock of the plant. Then you removed the dead leaves and your hostas went to ground for their winter rest. What you had probably not realised was that under those dying leaves, slugs and snails found the ideal protective humid nesting ground, and had been happily reproducing and burying their eggs in the soil at the base of your hostas.

When spring arrives and you diligently and speedily put your barriers around the newly emerging hosta shoots, you are just succeeding in trapping the eggs which will then hatch out to find they have been born in hosta heaven! What you should do, as soon as you see sign of the spring shoots, is remove and dispose of a ring of egg-laden soil, 2" deep and 12" in diameter from around the plants. Replace this immediately with fresh compost and your chosen slug and snail prevention. Job done!

Give an aged look to rocks with some friendly bacteria

Newly acquired rocks added to an existing rockery, or new bricks used to repair an old wall can stick out like a sore thumb until they have weathered for a year or so. You can easily speed up this aging process with nothing more than a pot of natural 'live' yoghurt and a roll of cling film, which is best done when the weather is warm. Paint the rock or brick surface with a generous layer of the yoghurt, which must be 'live' as this contains the mix of bacteria that holds the key to this tip working. Next completely cover the yoghurt painted surface with cling film and just wait. After about two weeks remove the cling film and wash off the remaining yoghurt. Amazingly the stone surface will have a dark weathered look and be home to algae and maybe even some lichen.

Pastry bird feeders – a real tweet!

Don't throw away any pastry off-cuts when baking. Mould them into different fun shapes (the kids will love to help!), press birdseed into the surface and make a hole for hanging before baking in the oven. The result is a selection of bird feeders to hang around the garden!

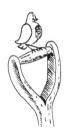

let them hunt for this rare spring bloom!

Here's a fun tip to amaze your friends! In the autumn choose a nice, plump daffodil bulb. Next buy from the greengrocer a large, fresh beetroot. Cut the top off the beetroot, hollow it out and mash up the scooped out material with one tablespoon of linseed oil. Next place the daffodil bulb inside the beetroot 'shell' and pack the mashed up beet around the bulb. Plant the whole thing in the garden, as you would a normal daffodil bulb. The result of your strange activity? Pink daffodil flowers in spring! Try it, but keep the admirers guessing as to how you did it. They will scour the garden centres for the elusive pink daffodil!

Spider plants love the dry life

You will often hear 'non-gardeners' say how easy they find spider plants to look after and boast that they always forget to water them and still they grow. Well, they have a point! Keep spider plants as dry as possible and you can't go wrong. Brown tips to the leaves are the first signs of over watering. As tempted as you are to include them in your regular watering regime, don't!

Free tomato plants!

When removing the first few side shoots from your tomato plants, don't throw them all in the compost bin. Instead, plant up some of them in 3" pots. They will easily root giving you plants to fill in any gaps and produce later fruits when the glut of summer fruit is over.

Borrow some pollen for a feast of fruit!

Not everyone has room for more than a couple of small fruit trees in their garden, and choosing them can be a headache because many varieties need the presence of another pollinating fruit tree in the vicinity. A neat way of getting round this problem is to find another garden in your area with the pollinating tree you require (nurseries will give you a list of suitable trees) and beg a sprig or two of flowering growth in spring. Put the ends of these pieces into a cut off plastic pop bottle of water and hang in your fruit tree. Amazingly the insects will pollinate your fruit flowers using the pollen from the introduced flowering stems!

Cut flowers can't compete with a bowl of fruit

If you have ever wondered why your vases of beautiful cut flowers don't last more than a few days, then take a look around the room. If you have a bowl of fruit anywhere – that is the reason. The gas (ethylene), which fruits give off as they ripen, will fade cut flowers very quickly. The further the distance the fruit is away from the flowers the longer the blooms will last!

Give the soil a hot bath before planting

Autumn is a good time to be planting new shrubs or moving existing ones around in the garden; root systems have a chance to develop before the plant comes back into full growth in spring. However, even autumn days can get really chilly and the soil temperature can drop considerably. To avoid the plant suffering a check to growth if the soil is chilled, soak the new planting hole with boiling water half an hour before planting – it makes all the difference!

Boiled egg water makes African Violets glow

If you have ever grown African violets then you will know that the flower colours can be wonderful. To make those bloom colours almost fluorescent the plant requires extra calcium. This can be given easily by watering the plants with the tepid water that you have just boiled eggs in! Enough calcium leaches out of the eggshells to make all the difference.

Oh dear! Another smelly tip!

Deer are best enjoyed at a distance, certainly not when they are ripping your prize plants to bits! Keeping deer, foxes and badgers out of your garden means resorting to something smelly. Strips of material soaked in creosote or household ammonia and hung in a net at the boundary point where you know these animals enter your garden will certainly do the trick. After a few weeks they will associate the area with the nasty smell and will avoid it long after you have got fed up with the smell yourself and stopped using the tip!

Clean off those pests with a soap spray

A multi-purpose, environmentally friendly plant spray against a range of pests can be made by saving up all those scraps of soap you have left. When you have enough, boil up 3 tablespoons of the soap bits with 1 gallon of water. When all of the soap has dissolved, allow the solution to cool and then give the affected plants a good spray. This should kill enough of the pests to give the plants a fighting chance.

A pretty deterrent for tomato whitefly

Get into the habit of always planting French marigolds alongside tomato plants – even in a hanging basket or window box. They will look very attractive and, more importantly, the smell given off by the marigolds will deter whitefly, a serious pest of tomatoes. The marigold variety 'Boy O Boy' works the best!

Shower caps are the tops for mini propagators

When staying in hotels how many people think to take the shower caps away with them? Not many. In fact remove the one from the bathroom each day and room service will leave you a new one. Collect as many as you can because these elasticated plastic caps make ideal propagator tops for large flowerpots. They are easy to take on and off and do away with the need for a plastic bag and an elastic band.

Bottles, buckets and bins give spray protection

If you really have to resort to chemical spraying for difficult weeds such as bindweed, mare's-tail and ground elder, then look to protect the surrounding plants from any spray drift, even on a still day. Bottomless plastic pop bottles of various sizes are good for small plant protection, with buckets and even plastic dustbins for the larger specimens. With systemic weed killers it only takes a little of the solution touching the leaves of a prize plant to cause heartbreaking results, so don't take the chance.

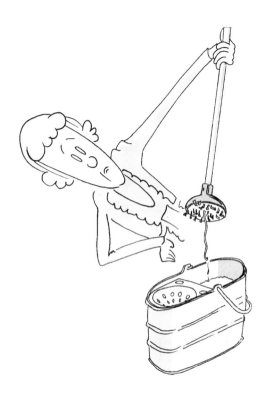

100s of uses for a cotton mop and each of them is a plant tie!

Next time you are walking past a skip have a peek inside and see if anyone has discarded an old cotton mop head. If so, beg it and you will have got yourself literally hundreds of free plant ties, each about 14" long. Soak the mop head in a weak bleach solution first, rinse and then get pulling!

Cyclamen are fussy but fun

Cyclamen make beautiful houseplants and are particular favourites at Christmas when they will flower continuously through the winter. The cyclamen plant grows from a surface-planted corm, which particularly resents being watered from above and will soon rot if treated in this way. It also prefers tepid water and high humidity (fussy little devil isn't it?!). Get into the habit of standing the plant pot in a saucer of wet clay granules and, when it requires watering, stand in a dish of warm water for about 10 minutes. It is worth the hassle, honestly!

Does that plant really need a soaking?

It is so easy to get the hose out and give everything in the garden a good drenching, but do all your plants need it? A few minutes spent having a feel of the compost in tubs, or the soil under leaves of plants in the border might just reveal some that are actually OK for water. Apart from saving water this might also save harming those plants that actually prefer it a bit on the dry side.

Hoe, hoe, hoe!

One of the most underrated and underused tools in the garden is the trusty old hoe. Hours of back breaking weeding can be avoided if you just spend a few minutes with a Dutch or flat hoe each week. Newly emerging weed seedlings have their lives cut short if you just hoe the top 1/2" of soil. This is best done in the sunshine so that the seedlings will wither and die quickly on the surface. Getting the hoe out early like this stops the weeds from producing seed, which they can do very quickly given the chance!

Steve's top 20 must-have wildlife attracting plants . . .

Allium hollandicum 'Purple Sensation' (Ornamental Onion)

Amelanchier lamarckii (Snowy Mespilus)

Aster novae-angelica (Michaelmas Daisy)

Berberis darwinii (Barberry)

Buddleia davidii (Butterfly Bush)

Cotoneaster 'Coral Beauty'

Digitalis species (Foxgloves)

Echinops species (Globe Thistle)

Eryngium species (Sea Holly)

Lavender angustifolia 'Hidcote' (English Lavender)

Lavander stoechas (French Lavender)

Malus 'Red Jade' (Weeping Crab)

Marjoram (Oregano)

Nepeta sibirica (Catmint)

Philadelphus 'Beauclerk' (Mock Orange)

Rosa (single) species (Dog Rose)

Salvia officinalis (Sage)

Santolina chamaecyparissus 'Small Ness' (Cotton Lavender)

Scabiosa species (Scabious)

Sedum spectabile (Ice Plant)

Soot can sweep away soil pests!

Many soil pests on the vegetable plot
can be deterred by raking soot into the
soil surface at sowing time. This works
particularly well for carrot root fly. If you
don't have an open fire yourself, then scrounge some from
a friend or neighbour. It'll be worth the effort.

A sooty watering gives radiant sweet peas

Whilst we are on the subject of soot, to intensify the colours of sweet pea flowers, water them around the roots with soot water when they are coming into bud.
The results are amazing!

Easy cuttings with Oasis cubes

Taking cuttings can be a tricky business with a tendency
for the plant material to get over watered and go rotten
before it has had a chance to make roots. Then there is
the trauma of transplanting which can cause major root
disturbance. Both these challenges can easily be met
by inserting the cutting into an inch square cube of wet
flower arranger's oasis. Keep the block moist and plant
the whole thing carefully into a pot at the first sign of roots
showing through the sides.

Rose, mint and garlic harmony!

Planting a combination of mint and wild garlic between
roses has a double benefit. The invasive mint smothers
any weeds, and the garlic emits a smell that deters
greenfly. Incredibly the three types of plants seem to grow
quite happily together.

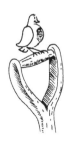

Steve's recipe for a perfect wildlife tapestry hedge . . .

This mixed hedge gives all round interest and colour for you and the wildlife. The recipe itself is mouth-watering and the result should be breathtaking!

Crataegus monogyna (Common Hawthorn)
Corylus avellana (Common Hazel)
Fagus sylvatica (Common Beech)
Fagus sylvatica 'Pupurea' (Copper Beech)
Cornus sanguinea OR *Cornus mas* (Flowering Dogwood)
Ilex aquifolium 'Argentea marginata' (Female Holly)
Ilex aquifolium 'Atlas' (Male Holly)
Prunus spinosa 'Pupurea' (Blackthorn)
Rosa rugosa 'Alba' OR *Rosa* 'Scabrosa' (Hedging Rose)
Hedera helix (Common Ivy - get two vigorous varieties, one plain and one-variegated)

Trimmed once a year in late winter, before the birds start nesting, this hedge will give you, and nature, years of pleasure.

Citrus appeal lures slugs and snails

Slug pellets are fast becoming a real no-no for the environmentally concerned gardener. If you can catch slugs and snails you can remove them from your garden. A good way of doing this is to place hollowed out half shells of large oranges and grapefruits around the borders in the evening. During the night the smell of the fruit will lure the slimy pests inside where they will remain waiting for you to collect them in the morning. This also encourages you to eat more fruit, which isn't a bad thing!

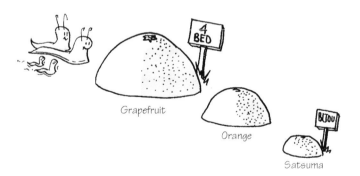

Grapefruit

Orange

Satsuma

Gardening diary is the key to success

How often do you begin a new gardening year with the memories of the successes and failures of the previous year fading fast? Recording all your gardening achievements and cock-ups with a camera and a diary makes next year's planning much easier. Do this throughout the season and be sure to make a note of sowing times, weather conditions etc… You can then review everything on a cold January evening and recall the joys of the previous summer!

Lime-hating plants love a good pine mulch

The key with keeping lime-hating plants looking good is to acidify the soil. Special liquid feeds will do this but a good, natural way is to mulch around the plants with dead pine needles. Collect these on your weekend walks in the park and put them to good use around your rhododendrons, azaleas etc…

Wet grass to cut? Cooking oil is all you need

Mowing the lawn when the grass is a bit damp can be a nightmare and cleaning the mower can take longer than the initial task. Avoid wet grass sticking by lightly spraying the blades and underside of the lawnmower with cooking oil before you mow. Amazingly the wet grass will not stick! Oil and water, you see, do not mix and the grass just drops off. Be sure to remove the oil with WD-40 before you cut dry grass or the opposite will happen!

Flat lemonade puts the fizz into cut flowers

Forget the fancy food you can buy to mix with water to keep your cut flowers fresh in the vase. Flat lemonade does the trick just as well! Be sure the lemonade is completely flat, as carbonated drink will not work as well. The sugars and other minerals in the flat lemonade really help to keep the blooms looking good.

Steve's top 20 slug and snail proof perennials . . .

Aconitum carmichaelii 'Arendsii'

Allium 'Globemaster' (Ornamental Onion)

Artemesia ludoviciana (Western Mugwort)

Arum italicum 'Marmoratum' (Lords and Ladies)

Aster ericoides 'Esther'

Bergenia species (Elephant's Ears)

Campanula percicifolia (Peach-leaved Bellflower)

Colchium 'Waterlily' (Autumn Crocus)

Corydalis lutea

Epimedium pinnatum (Barrenwort)

Galanthus species (Snowdrop)

Geranium macrorrhizum (Cranesbill)

Helleborus foetidus (Bear's Foot)

Helleborus x nigercors

Hosta 'Halcyon' (Plantation Lily)

Iris chrysographes

Lobelia siphilitica (Blue Cardinal Flower)

Pulmonaria angustifolia (Blue Cowslip)

Rudbeckia hirta (Black-eyed Susan)

Sedum telephium 'Matrona' (Ice Plant)

Pop on a plastic bottle for perfect protection!

Always have a supply of homemade individual cloches handy for those late frost emergencies. To make them, simply save empty, clear plastic pop bottles of various sizes and cut off the bottoms. Place over the tender plants and push a little way into the soil. Remember to screw the lid on at night but remove it during the day.

DON'T FORGET TO CUT OFF THE
BOTTOM OF THE BOTTLE!

Keep your wellies bug-free!

It's happened to every gardener at some time – you pull on your wellies only to feel the telltale wriggle of that huge spider that has taken up residence in the toe end! Avoid this nightmare by simply covering your wellingtons with a pair of tights immediately after taking them off.

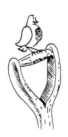

Now here's a wee tip!

If you want your compost heap to rot down really quickly and produce some tip-top compost, then male urine is what you want! Collect in a bottle, pour onto the heap immediately and mix into the top 6" layer. It seems that there are chemicals, present only in male urine, which speed up the breakdown of plant material. Sorry ladies! Can't use you here!

Temper, temper!

Never prune in a bad mood! Pruning is one of those tasks for which you need to feel relaxed and at one with yourself and the plants around you, letting the kind, gentle hand of Mother Nature guide your every cut with exquisite perfection. If you're in a strop you'll just chop the lot down!

Index by Problem

Index by Solution

T

U

V

W

Y

Index of Steve's favourites

Notes

Notes

'The Greatest Tips in the World' series . . .

Also available:

ISBN 1-905151-02-0
Pub Date: Sept 2005

ISBN 1-905151-03-9
Pub Date: Sept 2005

ISBN 1-905151-04-7
Pub Date: Sept 2005

ISBN 1-905151-05-5
Pub Date: Sept 2005

ISBN 1-905151-01-1
Pub Date: April 2006

ISBN 1-905151-09-8
Pub Date: April 2006

ISBN 1-905151-08-X
Pub Date: April 2006

ISBN 1-905151-07-1
Pub Date: April 2006

ISBN 1-905151-11-X
Pub Date: Sept 2006

ISBN 1-905151-12-8
Pub Date: Sept 2006

ISBN 1-905151-13-6
Pub Date: Sept 2006

With many more to follow, these books will form a most useful compilation for any bookshelf.

Other 'The Greatest in the World' products . . .

DVDs

'The Greatest Gardening Tips in the World' - presented by Steve Brookes
(release date: September 2005)

'The Greatest Cat Tips in the World' - presented by Joe Inglis
(release date: September 2006)

'The Greatest Dog Tips in the World' - presented by Joe Inglis
(release date: September 2006)

'The Greatest Golfing Tips in the World' - Vols. 1 & 2 - presented by
John Cook (release date: September 2006)

'The Greatest Yoga Tips in the World' - presented by David Gellineau and
David Robson (release date: September 2005)

'The Greatest Cat Cuisine in the World' - presented by Joe Inglis
(release date: September 2006)

'The Greatest Dog Cusine in the World' - presented by Joe Inglis
(release date: September 2006)

Hardback, full-colour books:

'The Greatest Cat Cuisine in the World' - by Joe Inglis
ISBN 1-905151-14-4 (publication date: September 2006)

'The Greatest Dog Cuisine in the World' - by Joe Inglis
ISBN 1-905151-15-2 (publication date: September 2006)

For more information about currently available and forthcoming book and
DVD titles please visit:

www.thegreatestintheworld.com

or write to:
Public Eye Publications
PO Box 3182
Stratford-upon-Avon
Warwickshire CV37 7XW
United Kingdom

Tel / Fax: +44(0)1789 299616
Email: info@publiceyepublications.co.uk

The Author

Steve Brookes is a fun, charismatic and experienced TV / radio presenter and journalist. His enthusiastic approach and subtle humour blend with his extensive horticultural knowledge to create a unique gardening personality. Steve's approach makes the subject rich and inspiring with both novice and experienced gardeners being informed and entertained as he introduces them to innovative ideas to make gardening enjoyable and rewarding.

Steve has won the prestigious Garden Writers' Guild award for the 'Best Radio Gardening Programme' and he also presented the successful Channel 4 series 'Growing Plants', which won the highly prized Royal Television Society award. He currently co-presents a regular gardening programme for BBC Radio and writes for the gardening press. Steve's writing is always from the heart and reflects his thoughts on a subject that has been his passion for many years.